W9-ACH-280

Cool
PET TREATS

Easy Recipes for Kids to Bake

Pam Price

ABDO
Publishing Company

Visit us at www.abdopublishing.com

Published by ABDO Publishing Company, 8000 West 78th Street, Edina, Minnesota 55439. Copyright © 2010 by Abdo Consulting Group, Inc. International copyrights reserved in all countries. No part of this book may be reproduced in any form without written permission from the publisher. Checkerboard Library™ is a trademark and logo of ABDO Publishing Company.

Printed in the United States of America, North Mankato, Minnesota
092009
012010

PRINTED ON RECYCLED PAPER

Editor: Liz Salzmann
Series Concept: Nancy Tuminelly
Cover and Interior Design: Anders Hanson, Mighty Media, Inc.
Photo Credits: Anders Hanson, Shutterstock

The following manufacturers/names appearing in this book are trademarks: Lunds & Byerly's®, Pyrex®

Library of Congress Cataloging-in-Publication Data

Price, Pamela S.
  Cool pet treats : easy recipes for kids to bake / Pam Price.
      p. cm. -- (Cool baking)
  Includes index.
  ISBN 978-1-60453-777-2
  1. Dogs--Feeding and feeds--Recipes--Juvenile literature. 2. Cats--Feeding and feeds--Recipes--Juvenile literature. I. Title.
  SF427.4.P75 2010
  636.7'085--dc22
                                2009029851

Table of Contents

Baking Is Cool

When it comes to baking, your pets don't have to be left out!

Animal trainers have a very handy tool in their bag of tricks. Treats! Treats reward animals for learning new behaviors and tricks. You could easily buy pet treats at a pet supply store. So, why make your own?

When you make treats yourself, you control the ingredients. You know that your pet is getting human-quality food instead of unknown ingredients. Plus, it's just plain fun to bake pet treats!

Your pet will love the treats you make from the recipes in this book. Just remember to limit the treats that you give to your pet. Like people, animals that eat too many treats will gain weight. Make sure that your pet gets plenty of exercise. Then your pet can be healthy and enjoy some of your treats!

GET THE PICTURE!

When a step number in a recipe has a colored circle around it, look for the picture that goes with it. The circle around the photo will be the same color as the step number.

1 →

Ready, Set, Bake!

Preparation is a key element of successful baking. Here are some things to keep in mind.

ASK PERMISSION

> Get permission to use the kitchen, baking tools, and ingredients.

> If you'd like to do something by yourself, say so. As long as you can do it safely, do it!

> Ask for help when you need it. Professional chefs have *sous chefs*, which means "assistant chefs" in French. You can have one too!

BE PREPARED

Read the whole recipe the day before you plan to bake.

> Make sure you have all the ingredients. Do you need to go to the grocery store?

> Will there be enough time? Sometimes dough needs to chill before you form it into a crust or cookies.

When it's time to bake, these steps will help you be organized.

> Gather all the tools and equipment you will need.

> Prepare the pans as directed and preheat the oven.

> Gather the listed ingredients. Sometimes you need prepared ingredients such as chopped nuts or sifted flour. Do those prep jobs as you gather the ingredients.

> Finally, do the recipe steps in the order they are listed.

Safety First!

When you bake you need to use an oven. Sometimes you also have to use sharp tools. Ask an adult helper to be in the kitchen with you. Here's how to keep it safe.

HOT STUFF

> Set up a cooling rack ahead of time.

> Make sure it's easy to get from the oven to the cooling area. There should be no people or things in the way.

> Always use oven mitts, not towels, when handling hot pots and pans.

> The oven is hot too. Don't bump into the racks or the door.

THAT'S SHARP

> Choose a small knife. Cut just a small amount of food at a time.

> Always keep your other hand away from the blade.

> Work slowly and keep your eyes on the knife.

SUPER SHARP!

In this book, you will see this symbol beside some recipes. It means you need to use a knife for those recipes. Ask an adult to stand by.

Germ Alert!

It's so tempting, but you shouldn't eat raw dough that contains eggs. Raw eggs may contain salmonella **bacteria**, which can cause food poisoning. Eating raw cookie dough that contains eggs might make you sick. Really sick! Ask an adult if it's okay to lick bowls, beaters, and spoons.

KEEP IT CLEAN

> Tie back long hair.

> Wash your hands before you begin baking. Rub them with soap for 20 seconds before rinsing. Wash them again if you eat, sneeze, cough, take a bathroom break, or touch the trash container.

> Use clean tools and equipment. If you lick a spoon, wash it before using it again.

> Make sure that your cutting board hasn't had raw meat on it.

Tools of the Trade

These are the basic tools used for baking pet treats. Each recipe in this book lists the tools you will need.

MEASURING
CUPS

MEASURING
SPOONS

KNIFE AND
CUTTING BOARD

MIXING BOWLS

SMALL SAUCEPAN

FORK

DINNER SPOON

WHISK

ROLLING PIN

TEA KETTLE

WOODEN SPOON

BISCUIT CUTTER OR COOKIE CUTTER

CAN OPENER

SPATULA

BAKING SHEET

Right Size It!

Cooking stores have all kinds of animal-themed cookie cutters. If you have a small pet, choose a small cookie cutter. Or, you can break larger treats into small pieces for your pet. Remember, cool cookie cutters are fun for us. Our pets don't care what shape their treats are. They just want to eat them!

OVEN MITTS

Convection Ovens

Is there a setting on your oven marked *convection*? Lucky you! Convection ovens have a fan that **circulates** the hot air in the oven. That makes food bake faster and more evenly. If you use a convection oven, reduce the temperatures given in the recipes by 25 degrees and reduce the baking times by about one-fourth or one-third.

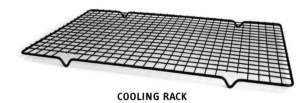

COOLING RACK

Cool Ingredients

You can find all the ingredients in this book at a grocery store. In fact, you can even taste the baked treats yourself. You just might not be as thrilled with them as your dog or cat will be!

FLOUR AND GRAINS

In a recipe, the word *flour* means all-purpose wheat flour. All-purpose flour is made with only the middle part of the wheat kernel. Whole-wheat flour contains the entire wheat kernel.

Wheat germ is the inner portion of the wheat kernel. It contains a lot of **vitamins** and **minerals**. Keep opened containers of wheat germ in the refrigerator.

Cornmeal is dried corn that's been ground to a medium **texture**. Corn flour, on the other hand, is ground to a fine texture. Cornmeal and corn flour are very different. Make sure you use the one the recipe calls for.

Rolled oats are oats that have been flattened by a heavy roller. In the grocery store, they may be called old-fashioned oatmeal. If a recipe calls for rolled oats, don't use quick oats or instant oatmeal. It will change the texture of what you're baking.

Keeping Your Pet Safe

Pets can eat most foods that we eat. But some foods can make them very sick, or even kill them. Do not feed these foods to your pets:

Dogs should not eat	Cats should not eat
➤ chocolate	➤ chocolate
➤ onion	➤ onion
➤ garlic (small amounts are okay)	➤ garlic (small amounts are okay)
➤ grapes	➤ grapes
➤ raisins	➤ raisins
➤ macadamia nuts	➤ macadamia nuts
➤ active dry yeast	➤ milk (but yogurt is okay)
➤ avocado	➤ mushrooms

Play it safe the first time you make treats for your pet. Show the recipe to your veterinarian. Ask if it's okay to feed the treats to your pet.

YEAST

The recipes in this book call for two different types of yeast. Brewer's  yeast is inactive yeast that some people add to food to get more **nutrients**. Dogs should not eat active dry yeast, but brewer's yeast is good for their skin and fur.

Active dry yeast is a **leavening** agent. Bakers use it to make bread and other baked goods rise. It's okay for cats to eat both kinds of yeast.

MILK

You can use whatever milk you have, whether it is skim, low fat, or whole milk. Substituting usually won't noticeably affect the quality of what you're making.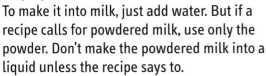

Powdered milk is milk that is **evaporated** until only a powder remains. To make it into milk, just add water. But if a recipe calls for powdered milk, use only the powder. Don't make the powdered milk into a liquid unless the recipe says to.

Milk causes digestive problems in many cats. Pet treat recipes that include milk should be fed only to dogs.

EGGS

Eggs come in many sizes. Use large eggs unless the recipe says 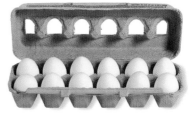 otherwise. Bring eggs to room temperature before you add them to the dough.

BUTTER AND VEGETABLE OIL

Always choose unsalted butter for baking. You add salt in most recipes. Using unsalted butter keeps the dough from having too much salt.

Vegetable oil is made by pressing seeds or other plant parts under high pressure. Some vegetable oils, such as olive oil, are very good for you. However, olive oil has a strong taste that makes it a poor choice for baking. Canola oil has a very light taste and is a good choice for most baking and cooking.

Some vegetable oils, such as linseed oil and tung oil cannot be eaten at all. Other vegetable oils, such as palm oil and coconut oil, contain fat that is bad for the heart.

CHEESE AND YOGURT

Cheese and yogurt are both made with milk. Usually the milk comes from cows, sheep, or goats. Different cheeses have different flavors and **textures**. The flavor and texture depend on the ingredients used. They also depend on how the cheese is made.

Yogurt is made by adding certain **bacteria** to milk. The milk becomes thick and slightly sour tasting.

FRUITS, VEGETABLES, AND HERBS

Fruits and vegetables are as good for your pets as they are for you! Always choose fruits and vegetables that are fresh and ripe.

Herbs, such as parsley and mint, add flavor and scent to foods. Catnip is related to mint.

PROTEIN-RICH INGREDIENTS

Cats and dogs are **carnivores**. Pet food companies process meat into powder for use in pet foods. So, treats made with fresh meat are extra special for your pets! Be sure that any meat you feed your pets is completely cooked.

Peanut butter has something in common with meat. They are both excellent sources of **protein**! Peanut butter is also a good source of **vitamins** and **minerals**.

Cool Techniques

These are the techniques that bakers use. If you can't remember how to do something, just reread these pages.

MEASURING DRY INGREDIENTS

Dip the measuring spoon or measuring cup into whatever you're measuring. Use a butter knife to scrape off the excess.

MIXING DRY INGREDIENTS

Unless the recipe says otherwise, always stir the dry ingredients together first. Measure them into a bowl and stir them with a fork or a whisk.

BEATING EGGS

Break the eggs into a mixing bowl. Beat them with a mixer until the yolks and whites are completely mixed. You can also beat eggs with a whisk or a fork. Hold the bowl firmly at a slight angle. Stir the eggs with rapid, circular movements.

SEPARATING AN EGG

Rap the egg firmly on the countertop. Hold the egg over a bowl and pull the shell apart. Gently pass the egg back and forth between the pieces of shell. The white will fall into the bowl. The yolk will remain in the shell.

GREASING A BAKING SHEET

There are several ways to grease a baking sheet. One is to wipe the pan with the butter wrapper. There's usually just enough butter left on it. You can also use a paper towel to rub butter on the pan. Or you can line it with parchment paper or a silicone mat.

KNEADING DOUGH

Place the dough on a floured surface. Place the heels of your hands on the dough. Push down and away from yourself. Fold the dough in half and give it a quarter turn. Press the heels of your hands into the dough again. Keep folding, turning, and pressing the dough until it is smooth and shiny.

ROLLING OUT DOUGH

Shape the dough into a disc. Place it on a floured countertop or pastry cloth. Roll the dough in one direction. Turn the dough or the rolling pin and roll in another direction. Continue rolling in different directions until the dough is the right thickness.

If you are using a cookie cutter, dip it in flour. Then cut out treats from the dough. After you cut out as many as you can, gather up the dough scraps. Form another disc of dough and roll it out. Cut out more treats. Repeat this process until you've used all the dough.

COOKING BACON

You can cook bacon in a microwave oven. Put a few paper towels on a plastic or ceramic plate. Put the bacon on the paper towels. Put three more paper towels over the bacon. Cook on high power for 3 minutes.

You can also cook bacon in the oven. Preheat the oven to 400 degrees. Place the bacon on a baking sheet. Bake for about 15 minutes.

Word Order Counts!

Pay attention to word order in the ingredients list. If it says "1 cup sifted flour," that means you sift some flour and then measure it. If the list says "1 cup flour, sifted," that means you measure first and then sift. Believe it or not, this makes a difference. Sifted flour is fluffier than unsifted flour. This means less of it fits in the measuring cup.

Canine Cheddar Cornbread

MAKES ABOUT
3 DOZEN TREATS

This cornbread will turn your dog into a chowhound!

INGREDIENTS

- 1 cup rolled oats
- ⅓ cup butter, cut into small pieces
- 1 cup boiling water
- ¾ cup cornmeal
- 1 tablespoon sugar
- 2 teaspoons chicken or beef instant bouillon
- ½ cup milk
- 4 ounces cheddar cheese, shredded (about 1 cup)
- 1 egg, beaten
- 2 cups flour

TOOLS: baking sheet | tea kettle | measuring spoons | biscuit cutter or | cooling rack | spatula
mixing bowl | measuring cups | wooden spoon | cookie cutter | oven mitts

1 Grease a baking sheet and set it aside. Preheat the oven to 325 degrees.

2 Put the rolled oats, butter, and boiling water in a mixing bowl. Stir to mix. Let the mixture stand for 10 minutes to soften the oats.

3 Add the cornmeal, sugar, bouillon, milk, cheese, and egg. Stir until everything is well mixed.

4 Add the flour a cup at a time. The dough will become very stiff and hard to stir.

5 Put the dough on a lightly floured surface. Knead it until it is smooth and no longer sticky. This will take several minutes.

6 Use your hands to pat the dough until it is ½ inch thick all over. Dip a 2-inch biscuit cutter or a cookie cutter in flour. Cut out the treats. For a small dog, flatten the dough to ¼ inch thick and use a smaller cutter. Space the treats about an inch apart on the baking sheet.

7 Bake the treats until they are browned, about 35 to 45 minutes. Small treats will take less time than large treats. Transfer the treats to a cooling rack. Let them cool completely.

Tasty Turkey Treats

Your dog will gobble up these tasty treats!

MAKES ABOUT
5 DOZEN TREATS

INGREDIENTS

- 1 pound ground turkey
- 2 tablespoons grated parmesan cheese
- 1 tablespoon parsley, finely chopped
- 2 eggs, beaten
- 2 tablespoons vegetable oil
- 2 cups whole-wheat flour
- 2 tablespoons brewer's yeast

TOOLS: mixing bowl · measuring cups · measuring spoons · small knife · cutting board · wooden spoon · baking sheets · cooling rack · oven mitts · spatula

1 Preheat the oven to 350 degrees.

2 In a large mixing bowl, combine the turkey, cheese, and parsley. Mix well. Stir in the eggs and oil.

3 Add the whole-wheat flour and brewer's yeast. Use your hands to work the flour into the meat mixture. Stop when the dough is smooth and completely mixed.

4 Roll small pieces of dough into balls. Place them about an inch apart on an ungreased baking sheet.

5 Bake the treats for about 20 minutes or until they are nicely browned. Let the treats cool on the baking sheet for about 3 minutes. Then move them to a cooling rack. Let them cool completely. The treats will harden as they cool.

Peanut Butter Pooches

MAKES ABOUT 2 DOZEN LARGE TREATS

Pooches love peanut butter. Woof, woof!

INGREDIENTS

- 1½ cups whole-wheat flour
- ½ cup flour
- ½ cup cornmeal
- ½ cup rolled oats
- ½ cup water
- ½ cup vegetable oil
- 2 eggs, lightly beaten
- 3 tablespoons peanut butter
- 1 teaspoon vanilla

TOOLS:

mixing bowl	whisk	cookie cutter
measuring cups	wooden spoon	baking sheets
measuring spoons	rolling pin	oven mitts

1. Preheat the oven to 350 degrees. Grease two baking sheets and set them aside.

2. Whisk together the two kinds of flour, cornmeal, and rolled oats in a large mixing bowl.

3. Make a well in the center of the dry ingredients. Put the water, oil, eggs, peanut butter, and vanilla in the well. Stir with a wooden spoon until mixed.

4. Lightly flour a countertop. Form the dough into a disk and place it on the floured surface. Roll it out until it is about ¼ inch thick. Cut out the treats with a cookie cutter. Place them about an inch apart on the baking sheets.

5. Gather up the dough scraps, form them into a disc, and roll out the dough again. Keep gathering up the scraps and rolling them out until you use all the dough.

6. Bake the treats for 10 minutes. Then open the oven and reverse the cookie sheets. That means move the upper cookie sheet to the lower rack. Move the lower cookie sheet to the upper rack. Bake for 10 more minutes.

7. Turn off the oven and let the treats cool in the oven. They will turn hard as they cool.

Bacon Bites

Your pup will beg for Bacon Bites!

MAKES ABOUT
4 DOZEN
TREATS

INGREDIENTS

6 slices bacon

4 eggs, beaten

2 tablespoons vegetable oil

1 cup water

½ cup powdered milk

2 cups flour

2½ cups wheat germ

TOOLS:
baking sheets
mixing bowl
measuring cups

measuring spoons
wooden spoon
2 dinner spoons

oven mitts

1 Preheat the oven to 350 degrees. Grease two baking sheets and set them aside for now.

2 Cook the bacon until it is crisp. When it is cool, crumble the bacon into small pieces.

3 Combine the crumbled bacon and the other ingredients in a mixing bowl. Stir with a wooden spoon to form a stiff dough.

4 Scoop up a small ball of dough with a spoon. Use a second spoon to push the dough onto the baking sheet. Place the balls of dough about 2 inches apart.

5 Bake the treats for 15 minutes. Turn off the oven and let them cool in the oven. They will harden as they cool.

Crazy Kitty Catnip Cookies

MAKES ABOUT 6 DOZEN TREATS

Is your kitty crazy for catnip?

INGREDIENTS

- ½ pound ground beef
- ¼ cup grated carrot
- 1 tablespoon shredded cheese
- 1 teaspoon active dry yeast
- 1 tablespoon dried catnip
- ½ cup plain bread crumbs
- 1 tablespoon tomato paste
- 1 egg, beaten

TOOLS:
baking sheet
mixing bowl
measuring cups
measuring spoons
cooling rack
spatula
oven mitts

24

1 Preheat the oven to 350 degrees. Grease a baking sheet and set it aside for now.

2 Put all of the ingredients in a large bowl. Stick in your hands and mush it all together.

3 Roll the mixture into small balls. Place them about an inch apart on the baking sheet. Bake the catnip cookies for about 15 minutes. They should be firm and lightly browned.

4 Transfer the catnip cookies to a cooling rack. Let them cool completely.

Cheesy Kitty Chews

MAKES MORE THAN
140 LITTLE TREATS

Your cat will
love these
simple treats!

INGREDIENTS

- ¾ cup shredded cheddar cheese
- ¼ cup grated parmesan cheese
- ¼ cup plain yogurt
- 1 egg, lightly beaten
- 1 tablespoon vegetable oil
- 1 tablespoon water
- ¾ cup flour
- ¼ cup cornmeal

TOOLS:
baking sheet
mixing bowl
measuring cups
measuring spoons
wooden spoon
small knife
oven mitts
cooling rack

1 Preheat the oven to 350 degrees. Grease a baking sheet and set it aside for now.

2 Stir together the cheeses, yogurt, egg, oil, and water. Stir in the flour and the cornmeal.

3 Cover your work surface and your hands with flour. Scoop up a small handful of dough. Roll it into a long, thin snake about ¼ inch thick. Cut off pieces about ½ inch long. Place them on the baking sheet. Bake the cheese treats for 15 minutes.

4 Put the baking sheet on a cooling rack. Leave the treats on the baking sheet until they are cool.

Terrific Tuna Tidbits

MAKES MORE THAN
140 LITTLE TREATS

INGREDIENTS

- 1 teaspoon vegetable oil
- 2 egg whites
- 1 5-ounce can of water-packed tuna
- ¼ cup cornmeal
- ½ cup whole-wheat flour

What cat doesn't like tuna!

TOOLS: measuring cups · measuring spoons · small saucepan · small knife · cutting board · can opener · mixing bowl · fork · rolling pin · baking sheet · cooling rack · oven mitts

1 Preheat the oven to 350 degrees.

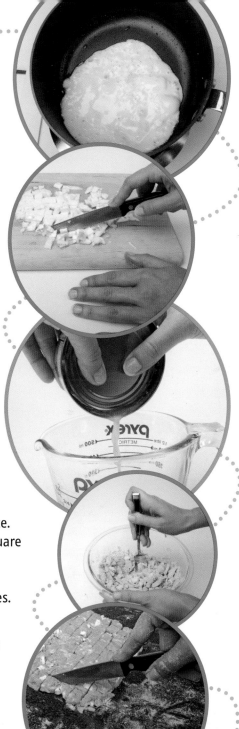

2 Heat the oil in a small saucepan over medium heat. Swirl the oil around to coat the bottom of the pan. Add the egg whites. Cook them without stirring until the egg whites are completely cooked.

3 Scrape the cooked egg whites onto a cutting board and let them cool. Then chop them into tiny pieces.

4 Open the can of tuna. Hold the can and loose lid upside down over a 1-cup measuring cup. Press the lid against the tuna. Squeeze all the tuna water into the measuring cup. You will need ¼ cup of tuna water. Add tap water to the tuna water if you don't have ¼ cup of tuna water.

5 Put the tuna in a mixing bowl. Use a fork or your fingertips to break the tuna into small pieces.

6 Add the tuna water and chopped egg white to the tuna. Stir the mixture with a fork. Stir in the cornmeal and flour.

7 Form the dough into a disc. Put it on a lightly floured surface. Sprinkle a little more flour over the dough. Roll it into a square about ¼ inch thick. Use a small knife to cut the dough into ½-inch squares. Place the squares close together on an ungreased baking sheet. Bake the tuna tidbits for 12 minutes.

8 Put the baking sheet on a cooling rack until the tuna tidbits are completely cool.

Wrap It Up!

Tips for keeping the treats you make fresh and delicious!

Each recipe in this book makes a lot of treats. Your pet shouldn't eat them all right away! So, keep most of the treats in the freezer. Put just a few treats in the refrigerator to give to your pet. When you run out, move a few more treats to the refrigerator. Always store the treats in plastic bags or airtight containers. Write the dates and types of treats on the outsides.

Some pets don't like cold food. Take a treat out of the refrigerator. After a couple of hours it will be room temperature. It's a perfect reward for a good dog or cat!

Homemade pet treats make great gifts. You can give them to friends when they get new pets. To wrap the treats, put them in a plastic bag. Then put that bag inside a gift bag with food-safe tissue paper.

Glossary

bacteria – tiny, one-celled organisms that can only be seen through a microscope.

carnivore – one who eats meat.

circulate – to move around, especially in a circular pattern.

evaporate – to change a liquid into a gas or solid by removing the water from it.

leavening – a substance such as yeast or baking soda that makes baked goods rise.

mineral – a natural element that plants, animals, and people need to be healthy.

nutrient – something that helps living things grow. Vitamins, minerals, and proteins are nutrients.

protein – a substance needed for good health, found naturally in meat, eggs, beans, nuts, and milk.

texture – how rough or smooth something looks or feels.

vitamin – a substance needed for good health, found naturally in plants and meats.

Web Sites

To learn more about cool baking, visit ABDO Publishing Company on the World Wide Web at **www.abdopublishing.com.** Web sites about cool baking are featured on our Book Links page. These links are routinely monitored and updated to provide the most current information available.

Index